Shifting TIMELINES

Co-Create an Extraordinary Life

CINDI JOHNSTON

BALBOA.
PRESS
A DIVISION OF HAY HOUSE

This book is a work of non-fiction. Unless otherwise noted, the author
and the publisher make no explicit guarantees as to the accuracy of
the information contained in this book and in some cases, names
of people and places have been altered to protect their privacy.

Balboa Press books may be ordered through booksellers or by contacting:

Balboa Press
A Division of Hay House
1663 Liberty Drive
Bloomington, IN 47403
www.balboapress.com
1 (877) 407-4847

Because of the dynamic nature of the Internet, any web addresses or
links contained in this book may have changed since publication and
may no longer be valid. The views expressed in this work are solely those
of the author and do not necessarily reflect the views of the publisher,
and the publisher hereby disclaims any responsibility for them.

The author of this book does not dispense medical advice or prescribe the use
of any technique as a form of treatment for physical, emotional, or medical
problems without the advice of a physician, either directly or indirectly. The
intent of the author is only to offer information of a general nature to help
you in your quest for emotional and spiritual well-being. In the event you use
any of the information in this book for yourself, which is your constitutional
right, the author and the publisher assume no responsibility for your actions.

Any people depicted in stock imagery provided by Thinkstock are
models, and such images are being used for illustrative purposes only.
Certain stock imagery © Thinkstock.

Print information available on the last page.

ISBN: 978-1-5043-8793-4 (sc)
ISBN: 978-1-5043-8794-1 (e)

Library of Congress Control Number: 2017914162

Balboa Press rev. date: 10/28/2017

DEDICATION

I dedicate this written creation to my mentor and friend, Jose Luis Herrera. Thank you for choosing to share your wisdom with us, your students and apprentices of the primordial medicine. Your refined teachings of this Ancient Knowledge truly are a part of the sacred seeding of the evolving Earth. May all who choose to walk with this lineage be as blessed as I have been since our pathways crossed.

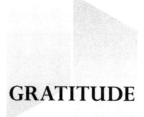

GRATITUDE

Thank you, Tina Thrussell, of Shin Dao Institute, for your immense wisdom and contribution to the sacred 'word'. Thanks to Jenny Cho for your graphic genius and endless patience. Thanks to Rebecka Freels, of Beyond Words Communication, for your longtime friendship and communication expertise. Thanks to my husband, Bob. You are always my rock when I need you most.

TABLE OF CONTENTS

INTRODUCTION

In this book, I refer to dialing into a radio station because I love the idea of influencing our own lives. I visualize the DJ who once operated with glazed eyes, following a prescribed play list for their life, ripping off their headphones and saying, "To heck with this! It's time for me to play what I want to play and dance how I want to dance!" Then I see the people of the world each waking up and beginning to live their authentic way, dancing to their own dance playlist.

I see the universe delivering the life and desires they want because they remember how to create the life they choose by using connections to alternate time lines.

Yes you, as the DJ of your life, can use the technology of alternate, or parallel, timelines - which are like radio stations that are all playing at once over the universal bandwidth.

Read on to discover how to develop your own unique playlist for your life by consciously choosing the radio stations – the timelines - you are dialing into. Select the songs – the energies – you want to hear and create the happy dance of your life!

There is a very intricate light body that surrounds each of us that is the conduit for personal magnetic information and vibration. Within this light body, there is a field of communication that connects us to an unseen vast cosmic web of information. We attract 'like vibration' through that web, based on our continual thoughts and the emotions we project into the world, both consciously and unconsciously. These thoughts and emotions are our personal vibrational signals that go out into the universe. Like, or similar, vibrational energies are then naturally returned to us with similar magnetic signatures through the universal law of attraction. Those energies connected to thoughts and emotions are the energetic seeds that we invisibly plant within the Earth Matrix, which then affect the physical manifestations that we experience in our day to day lives.

At a very basic level, upbeat thoughts and emotions being sent out from your personal energy field will then return upbeat experiences back to you, and negative vibrational energies will provide similar frequency based experiences. Everyone, including you, is in a constant energetic exchange with a very large universal energy grid that naturally fuels our experiences. In effect, you are the DJ of your life dialing into a cosmic band of radio stations that affects your life in ways you don't even see or know, but feel the intimate effect of every day.

A very powerful way to create your life is to tap into other timelines to draw forth the gifts from those timelines that would positively assist you in creating and manifesting the life you desire. Timeline management is how the magicians, alchemists and mystery school masters lived very sacred and powerful lives. They knew and understood how life was created here on Earth. Through their accessing of alternate timelines, they were able to positively influence their lives. You also have that ability to do the same if you choose to. It all boils down to the questions, "What radio stations are you choosing to tune into? Are these radio stations working for you, or do you need to change your stations?"

PART 1

Shifting Timelines

The Human Energetic Communication Field

Universal Forces

Universal Forces

This is a diagram showing the communication field that lies within a matrix of light filaments that surround every soul. This large light field is known as the light body. During a human incarnation on Earth, these filaments inter-weave within the communication fields directly affecting each person's daily life.

CHAPTER 1

The Evolution of Co-Creation

The world and the chaos that abounds with different factions of beliefs is in direct relationship with the fact that we, as a human race, are 'mental creators'. Somewhere in time, we used to be 'sensory creators', who operated from the heart. We would feel into a situation and then mentalize the desired outcome. Good experiences would follow because we were able to directly draw upon our own higher powers of innate feeling to shift our reality. In other words, we knew how to change our radio station.

Today we operate from a mental and emotional precept that often has no relationship with Source energy or our higher divine awareness. As a society of humans, we rarely communicate with our higher wisdom and our souls on a daily basis, unless we find ourselves in deep crisis. We have moved from knowing ourselves and our truth and deciding our course of action through our innate wisdom, to reacting to emotional stimuli through a limited ego construct that only draws conclusions from past experiences. Many people have become mental and emotional drama 'junkies' always waiting for bad to happen; ready to react accordingly, living either very offensively or defensively, rather than co-creatively.

Here is where the lovely tasting juice of life has turned sour. This unfortunate shift from the heart to the head has made us weak and vulnerable to outside emotional and thought based influences of others who don't always have our best interests in mind. We have become a species programmed to think in ways that support the big commerce machine, rather than ways that support ourselves. The flow of information is coming from the outside world rather than flowing from our innate selves that see and know much. Our world has become limited because we are sourcing from profound limitation. Bluntly stated, we have lost connection with our natural state of being. We have lost much of our power as sovereign beings.

This book reveals great news. The disempowered ways of the human being are about to change. We are coming back online. The metaphorical human computer that is innate and wise is firing back up. All the programs that used to operate behind the scenes to ensure that we were following our soul's wisdom will get louder and more pronounced. The time of the 'sleep walking' human is coming to an end. The 'divine human' is coming back on line. Those with greedy intentions to contain or reduce our masterful abilities to co-create a positive life are beginning to lose their influence.

Yes, it is true. The human race is now waking up due to unique cosmic influences that are shifting the Earth's frequency. We are about to begin shedding very old, disempowered ways of being that have been stored in our light body that held us in a suffering pattern. Soon, as these cosmic shifts continue to take place, we will begin to step into a co-creator position that feeds good experiences back into our lives. We will remember what we used to know before our divine amnesia became the norm. We will remember how to selectively choose the 'radio stations' we are tuning into. It is a profound and exciting time to be alive; a special time that we incarnated into for very specific reasons!

CHAPTER 2

The Existence of Parallel Time Lines

Parallel time lines, alternate realities, and parallel universes are terms used to describe a universal energy landscape that can stretch the human mind. I will use a visualisation to help put this all into perspective. Visualize for a minute, an ant living in an ant hill in the trees within New York's Central Park. The ant knows what is going on in his ant hill. He may even understand the areas of the park he travels to as he gathers resources, such as small crumbs of bread near his home. Yet the ant only knows what is going on in his vicinity of his life and the ant hill. He does not know about the cafe located across the street from Central Park. He is unaware of the humans who frequent this café to buy their vanilla lattes while they text a loved one who lives far away in Montana. The cafe, the latte, the text are all real and exist very close to the ant, but the ant is completely unaware of it all. This lack of awareness seriously limits the ant.

You and I are like the ants living in a small ant hill located in a very complex universal energy field that cannot be seen or understood. This energy field is very real and very challenging to define because it's almost too big to comprehend. However, our experiences can assist us in understanding that we do live in a very complex universe that has alternate timelines running simultaneously.

While I understand the concept of parallel time lines and how it works from a mystical and practical point of view, I am no quantum physicist on the leading edge of this new science that we are just beginning to understand. It's a challenge to try to explain from a microcosmic level how the macrocosm level operates, but I know from life's quirky experiences that parallel timelines are at play.

Examples will be the best way to lend understanding to how parallel timelines and realities intertwine within your own life. I think it's easier to give examples than to try to define the undefinable.

Have you ever been on the way to the kitchen to get something from the fridge and half way to your destination you stop and forget what you were going to get? Or perhaps you have gone to retrieve a file from your file cabinet, and once you find yourself standing in front of the files, you stare at them with a blank look, not remembering what file you came to retrieve. In both these examples, you likely remember what you came to do if you just stop for a minute and try to think it through.

What just happened? I believe that in some way, without your knowing it, you dialed out of the timeline you were in. Then you paused, took a breath and dialed back into the appropriate timeline.

Your consciousness sometimes travels the cosmos for brief seconds, and that is why you forget what you had planned to do. You step out of this timeline for the time that you have forgotten your plans, and then you step back in when you remember. I believe we are 'Timeline Shifting' in this way all the time, but often we are unaware that we are doing it. Sometimes we even 'Timeline Jump' into a timeline that is remarkably different from this timeline.

A great example of connecting with another timeline through a 'Timeline Jump' is when you meet someone whom you feel as if you know, even when you haven't met them before. The chances are you do know that person in another parallel experience. Some may refer to this type of example as a remembrance of a past life, but chances are that life wasn't in the past. That life is happening simultaneously, in a parallel time line. That is why the energy of knowing them is so strong.

This parallel timeline theory also explains why we have a sixth sense that the mind cannot deny. Many mystical experts suggest that all our lifetimes are happening at once, just like all the radio stations are playing at once. Like the ant who was unaware of the café, the latte and the text, we don't know what is broadcasting on the other stations while we are focused on listening to this one in the here and now.

I used to be a big believer of past lives only, but now I subscribe to both ideas. I believe we have stored, within our light bodies, past life information from other incarnations. I also believe there are simultaneous lives occurring at the same time as this incarnation, interacting with this life. I believe the soul decides to project itself into more than one physical life form at once.

This idea of simultaneous lives has caused me to stretch myself. I have had some very unusual experiences during my 18 years studying and working within these mystical fields. These unique experiences I've had suggest we are living in a universal broadcast scenario where we can be intimately involved in more than one physical life. In a weird, soap opera type way, we are weaving together multiple physical experiences all at once.

The key to the example of knowing someone you've never met before is acknowledging that you usually have more than a sense that you know this person; you also know whether you like them or not. It may make no sense to your mind. How can you know whether you like them or not when you've never met them? You have sensory information that is generating a real feeling, and it is an important indication that something mystical is happening.

This idea then leads to the question, "Why would you meet them again in this lifetime if you are already experiencing them in another timeline?" My simple answer is because something you are learning in another timeline with that relationship must also be learned in this reality. Or another option is that you are just not getting the lessons in that other timeline, and this life timeline experience can give you another shot at it. The soul needs fulfilment, and the soul has a plan. If the plan is not going well in that other timeline, that plan may need to spill into this timeline as well. This duplication of experiences can give you a second chance at the same issues that you are meant to overcome.

It may be a stretch to accept this idea, but in my years of the mystical experience, it has been the case with clients I have worked with before. I have been witness to some pretty dramatic stories showing up during our sessions when I intuitively tracked the cause of their unhealable wounds. Sometimes I saw things that did not make sense to this timeline. I have seen people living on other planets experiencing similar challenges in both timelines. I have seen a female client who shows up as a male in another timeline. That client was living similar circumstances in the other timeline but from an opposite sex perspective.

I have also seen my human clients showing up as non-human beings or aliens in other timelines. It may be hard to believe this alien scenario, but I have intuitively seen some very bizarre and unique landscapes that were not from Earth, and the person I was sitting with had been influenced by their parallel, out of this world, experience.

This is why sometimes you meet people that don't seem to fit here on Earth; their behaviours are unique and different from the norm. Perhaps, as a soul, this is the first experience they've had here on Earth, and it's causing them some challenges. Often the most proficient way to assist my clients in healing is to bring the details of a parallel life forward and allow them to emotionally and mentally mingle with those details. When I make them aware of what was running in their background, without their everyday awareness, there is usually an emotional release that is related to both timelines. This release allows for permanent healing. I have seen miraculous outcomes for my clients because we tended to the healing of another timeline that was impacting this one. You see, we are very complex beings living in a very complex multi-verse.

I have been very lucky to consciously experience a simultaneous timeline while I was still experiencing this one. In early 2017, I sat with a plant medicine shaman in South America and during that profound experience I was able to access more than one timeline simultaneously with the assistance of the plant medicine spirits. The plant medicines we ingested during ceremony allowed me to consciously unhook from this reality. I was able to intentionally open doorways to other timelines and look inside them. It was a life altering experience, to say the least.

My elderly father passed away in early 2016, and even though I had sat with him in dream time, and would have intuitive messages come through from him, I never saw him with my own eyes after he passed. While journeying with the ayahuasca in my system, with my eyes open, I was able to see the room I was sitting in with all the details of the ceremony. When I closed my eyes, I would see other details connected to other experiences that were part of other timelines. While my eyes were closed, it was like I was watching an internal mind movie and I was able to change stations as I asked questions in my mind. My questions were the radio channel changer. Each question would create a different answer that would unfold in my mind movie. I did four ceremonies on that trip, and each ceremony provided different information. Sometimes I saw lots of details and other times I just heard words explaining things to me.

In the last ceremony, my mom popped into my mind movie while my eyes were closed. My mom had died in 1999 so she has been gone for a long time from my current timeline. She began to speak to me about the details of my life and what I needed to focus on. She spoke about my husband, my son and my sister. She was supporting me as a loving mother would. When she was finished speaking with me, I asked her about my dad. She told me to open my eyes and look up. I opened my eyes and saw Jerry, one of the leaders of the ceremony, standing by the fire sweeping ashes. I closed my eyes and said, "Dad is not here."

She told me very simply, "Open your eyes again." I opened my eyes again, after taking a really big, deep breath. I think I just needed to breathe deeper to solidify my physical presences in this time line. When I opened my eyes, I saw my father working on the fire. He had taken Jerry's position by the fire. While my father swept, he looked up at me and flashed a gentle smile, then he put his head down and went back to working the fire. It was my dad; it was his build and his way of moving. Jerry was a much thinner, younger man. I thought to myself, "Why isn't he coming over to talk to me?"

As I had that thought, I heard my mom call me back to my mind movie. I closed my eyes, and she continued to speak with me. I asked her why my father did not say anything and she told me because it wasn't possible for us to completely interact. As she spoke to me, tears flowed from my eyes, and I released some of my pent-up grief.

What was very interesting was that I knew there was a different timeline interaction that had just taken place. I almost sensed the radio station changing. I talked with Jerry after the ceremony, and he mentioned he'd had an unusual experience during that time, too. He was feeling very tired because of it. I think Jerry was impacted by the timeline opening up where he was standing; a full physical Timeline Jump can affect us physically. I cannot explain what happened during the ceremony from a logical place. I just know there was a switch of people and a timeline interweaving that I could see with my physical eyes because I was under the influence of a sacred plant medicine.

The experience of synchronicities can also be explained under the umbrella of parallel timelines. Let's use an example of a brilliant idea coming to you, and then suddenly you meet someone who can help bring your idea to light. The first question I would ask is, "Do you know where that idea might have originated?" You might respond that it came from your Higher Self, if you believe in a Higher Self. However, the web of the universe is much more complicated with multiple sources of stored information that may present themselves when necessary. I believe, in this example, there is an intricate, morphic field communication happening via your light body. An easy explanation is that somewhere in another timeline, you have already lived that idea and now you want to experience a plot twist, and the person who can help you bring that idea to life appears.

Here in this timeline is where you live something again in a similar, yet different way. All the components - such as people, places, and events - are lined up perfectly when the time is right for that required experience to unfold.

The opportunities and scenarios available to us at the morphic level are limitless. This is the world of creation that we struggle to understand. Just like the ant, unaware of what is going on beyond his conscious awareness, you may be unaware of what is going on beyond this timeline, but synchronicities are a sign that these parallel timelines do exist. Parallel timelines interact with you when the time is right for your required learning and evolution.

Synchronicity seems like a very magical thing, and the details behind the scenes must be mind-blowing. However, I relate synchronicity back to the soul and it's big, intricate, SOUL evolutionary plan that you are experiencing. In some complicated way, your soul orchestrates the link up of all the pieces needed for its next step when the time is right.

Other timelines intertwining with this one often happens, whenever we require specific experiences for growth. If you could imagine your soul as luminous weaving that has many fabrics weaved together to create this sacred cloth called you, then it makes sense that these parallel lives must intersect at certain times. There is a luminous communication going on that we, like little ants going about our business, cannot possibly understand, but it is real.

The phenomenon of déjà vu is the best example I can think of to show that parallel timelines exist. I believe déjà vu is a unique mixing of information within our communication body. I am unsure what triggers the unusual communication, but it's always a unique and obvious experience when déjà vu happens. Perhaps, déjà vu is where our simultaneous lifetimes intersect, like the threads of a soul weaving naturally to make the weaving stronger.

From my training and experience, I know there are 'veils' between timelines that create natural separation between the timelines. I sense there are also bridges made up of energy that allow us to access timelines as we need to or choose to. What I am noticing is the veils between timelines are thinning now. I suspect this change will allow us to access knowledge we have not been able to access in recent times.

While we focus our consciousness within a physical form, I am unsure if we can completely understand how our communication fields will work. I doubt we will fully understand until we die and shift our consciousness to another place in the multiverse where we awaken in the 'bigger perspective' reality, where all timelines are accessible. I believe death is just like the ant being plucked out of its limited perspective and transported above New York city in a spaceship so that he can see what he was a part of, beyond his limited 'ant hill' experience. I feel that the expansion of awareness is unbelievable at death. The plant ceremonies I did in South America gave me a glimpse into what I might experience at death and the word 'expansion' is the best word I have to explain it. Words are so limiting. I think you would have to experience such a ceremony for yourself to understand how vast your consciousness really is.

CHAPTER 3

Understanding our Divine Nature

We are divine beings, vast beyond our awareness, yet we are living in a very condensed reality. We are the 'big gift' stuffed in a very 'small box' called a physical body just waiting to be opened. I believe our true power comes when we unwrap our gifts through our understanding of how we truly operate in the world; when we fully understand that our thoughts and actions can either be beneficial or harmful to ourselves and others. Many humans have not figured out how powerful they are through their thought and spoken word; they tend to misuse their personal power through mental and emotional interactions.

In 2012, our divine evolution poked us to become even more conscious, to remember who we are and what our capacity is to create life in the most sacred of ways. I have been reminded many times to not ignore the metaphysical nature of life. I have had some great mystical experiences in my past. However, they were not always easy. Perhaps the purpose of those challenges was to teach me about my own personal power and how life really works. We do live in a divine matrix filled with infinite possibilities.

When I was a teenager, I was very psychic, but I didn't know how to manage my abilities. I have learned a lot over the years, and now, I am the manager of my experiences. Back then, I was a boat without a paddle, and the energetic world could sometimes toss me around in difficult ways. I was able to foretell things I was not comfortable foretelling, and I experienced a lot of déjà vu. I remember between the ages of 16 - 19 I would experience déjà vu often. Sometimes it would occur several times in one day. I would walk into a room, and I would experience everything as though I was rewinding a movie that I had already watched. It was disturbing if I saw things that I didn't like.

It was very uncomfortable when I had strange experiences I could not share with others. My parents always diverted the subject when I tried to talk to them about what I experienced. I look back to my younger years, and I know now I was learning about the unseen influences that can impact how we think and how we feel.

The experience of déjà vu was the most powerful of teachers. Have you ever played the game *Waldo* where you compare two pictures that seem exactly alike to the untrained eye? Upon closer investigation, you notice there are slight differences between the pictures. I have had that happen during a déjà vu experience. I know when I walked into that experience everything seemed the same, but something showed that was a little different and sometimes I would have to take a second or third look. The differences were subtle. Sometimes the colour of a person's shirt, or the colour of their eyes, would be slightly different. I would notice green eyes on a woman, and then when I looked at her again, her eyes were brown. This is a great example of how parallel time lines can sync up.

With all my metaphysical training - especially my shamanic training - I now understand that I have some active, energetic wiring that allows me to jump timelines and stay conscious. I can tune into more than one radio station and still experience the clarity and cognitive understanding of more than one signal. I believe my light body wiring is what created my many paranormal experiences and why I was drawn into this line of work. It's also why the study of metaphysics and the mystical traditions have been my main focus for so long. I wanted to understand the multiverse and how it has been influencing me my whole life. I also wanted to understand my extrasensory perceptions and how best to relate with my experiences in this current timeline.

I've had to work on dialing into the positive timelines connected to Earth, so that I would not be harmed by the negative timelines. My extensive training was needed to learn how to ensure I was able to do that.

The key is that both negative and positive timelines are accessible to everyone of us while living on Earth. This is why I want to share how to be your own DJ and dial into the appropriate station that you want to live by. Everyone on Earth has abilities to tap into other sources that can influence life!

I am grateful to the masters and scholars who came before me. They educated us on the light body and its unique communication patterns that allow us to access parallel time worlds. Their knowledge helped me understand what was going on for me, and showed me how to help others.

The parallel timeline effect has a far reaching influence and impact on our world and our experiences. I feel many mental illnesses are connected to Timeline Jumping and intertwining that goes on without our awareness. I think bipolar and schizophrenic conditions are related to the way a person's light body is energetically wired, and how their communication field is flowing with information. Anyone who has strong connections to the astral dimension but is not managing them may struggle. A person with multiple personality disorder, for example, is truly living those lives that they are channelling. It's hard for them to discern who they are, when they have so many multiple timelines spilling into this one.

I believe those diagnosed with apparent mental imbalance are often suffering from a form of parallel timeline disorder when too much information is flooding this timeline. I believe those with mental imbalance are missing natural veils that might normally block excess information leaking into this reality. Simply put, their filters are perhaps not working the way they should.

The parallel timeline effect needs to be studied more. I am hoping the quantum scientists will be able to make sense of the parallel timeline phenomena soon. It is my hope that by publishing this information, some brilliant doctors will choose to investigate further alternate realities and how they operate. Doctors who deal with mental disorders could sit with the plant shamans in South America so that they have their own direct experiences with multiple timelines. They could ask the multi-verse how to help people who struggle with these disorders. Perhaps then we can truly assist these people with their challenges.

I have wondered how many alternate timelines we might live in, and my intuitive guidance suggests it is limitless. If that's true, think about what that could mean for you as you choose to create your own life! It's pretty exciting to know you could access limitless 'songs' (parallel timelines) as you learn how to be the DJ of your life.

The idea of limitless parallel timelines opens up unbelievable next steps for the evolving human.

CHAPTER 4

Why the Soul Chooses to Live in Multiple Timelines

Parallel timelines are the soul's way of being an efficient 'evolver'. The soul is like a brand new baby who wants to live it all. The soul seeks to know itself and therefore may choose to experience multiple incarnations at once while gathering higher-self 'wisdom' from different life experiences. The more experiences we have, the quicker we will wake up and become wise and more Creator-like in physical form. All the clients I have met with in the past, and learned from, indicate that this is the soul's plan.

What seems to be a challenge, from my 'healer's perspective', is living difficult experiences in many timelines simultaneously. That type of overt 'to do list' - involving immense emotionally charged experiences - can seem to prohibit you from moving ahead and impede your evolution, at least in this timeline.

Many clients have come to see me with 'unhealable wounds'. They often sought out my services because there was something they could not get past, no matter what they did. In this case, the soul decides to take on too much, and the divine plan becomes burdensome. I truly believe when we, as souls, are on the other side planning out our incarnations, we forget how dense things can be here on planet Earth. It slips the soul's mind how Earth's timelines have stored lots of tough emotional history and how hard it can be at times to break free from the emotional and mental roller coaster we find ourselves on. The soul forgets how hard it can be to be a human being who is energetically tied to a big 'Human Collective' that informs us, whether we are aware of it or not.

All that emotion tied to other timelines can create messy circumstances. I have seen some pretty wild circumstances through the shamanic journeys I have done for clients. Some souls have chosen difficult paths for this lifetime and other lifetimes, at the same time. Sometimes it's like the fearful nightmare that just doesn't stop, and then, unfortunately, begins to spill into this lifetime. The over-spill can harm a person, rather than help them evolve. I have seen many suicidal people who present with what appears to be a really good life here, but they just can't see it. The other timelines where they are living out a hellish experience are spilling into this timeline, and it's too difficult to take. It's why suicide seems to be the only option to them, while the rest of the world judges them for what seems to be an unwarranted reaction. As a healer who has witnessed many unusual and difficult circumstances outside of the normal precept, I was reminded early on in my career to never 'judge a book by its cover'. The only way to truly understand what a soul is dealing with is to dig deep and leave no stone unturned.

I worked with a man once who could not face his 95-year-old mother's death. He was in huge denial about her death and could not understand why she died. Most people would have celebrated the age she made it to, but for him, it was unacceptable. I did some work with him around acceptance, but nothing eased his emotional upset. I decided, the second time we met, to go into a trance journey. I asked to see from a soul level what was running for him that was spilling into this life. At the time, back in 2006, I thought I was looking for a past life in which he had unfinished business. Now I know that what was happening for him was a parallel life spilling into this life, creating intense emotion.

During the journey I took on his behalf, I saw a young woman with young children riding a carriage pulled by horses. The mother was bounced out of the carriage and was run over by the heavy wooden carriage wheel. She sustained substantial internal injuries. I saw the same man I was working with in this timeline holding his wife, praying for her to stay and be with him as he watched her slowly pass away in his arms. That husband who had just lost his wife and the mother of his children was the same soul who had just lost his 95-year-old mother. His pain was overwhelming, and so was his inability to accept both deaths. During that healing session, I called forth that alternate timeline tragedy. I had him emotionally step into that carriage experience and step out of his mother's death experience. I was able to see the details of the accident, and as I shared the details with him, he became more and more emotional. I helped him turn his radio station to the source of his deepest pain. I helped him release those emotions first before we turned back to this timeline to help him release the emotions of his mother's death in this timeline. Both timelines were sinking him here in this lifetime, and yet, he knew nothing about the other timeline. Once he released both timeline traumas, his healing journey began. Re-solution started to take hold.

I talked with this client a few times after this session, and he had begun to grieve naturally. He was able to put things back into more balanced context.

I had another client whom I'd worked with around the theme of abandonment. In many timelines, she had experienced the theme of abandonment. In this lifetime, her husband had left her. Her marriage had ended before she was ready to let it go. She never seemed to be able to get over her husband's departure. For many years after her marriage ended, she hit low points and went back to the unhealed grief. She experienced overt depression when life challenged her and yet, in many ways, her life was going well. Unfortunately, she just couldn't change her radio station. Something unconscious was always drawing her back to experiencing loss and grief.

The last time I worked with her, before I retired as a healer, I saw a parallel timeline where her father died suddenly. She was unable to accept his death because she saw it as a tragic form of abandonment. Then a wonderful thing happened in that session. Her deceased father from that other timeline came through from the astral dimension and guided her to another perception and understanding, which helped her finally let go of her grief. Her father's spirit helped her unhook from that timeline theme that she had not healed from and helped her tune into some other radio stations where abandonment was not running.

What was interesting for me to witness, from a nonpersonal perspective, was the fact that the father in the alternate timeline was the same soul who represented her father in this lifetime. It was hard to distinguish who was speaking to her (through me). Was it this father who had died in this lifetime or the other father from another timeline who had died? She felt it was her father from this lifetime who was speaking to her, and I saw him as the other father from another timeline. In the end, it didn't matter who was speaking. She was able to release the low vibration of grief that was sitting in her light body and affecting how information flowed within her Human Energetic Communication Field. Both timelines healed when she was able to release her grief connected to both. The work was complete for her. The soul that she had unfinished business with was now healed.

Since that session, she has been in a very good space. She has done some amazing personal work to help herself stay upbeat. She is taking powerful steps to move her life forward.

The healing with her fathers from both timelines helped her close the door permanently to the old abandonment theme. This healing also closed the doors to the attached timelines that were causing her difficulty.

This experience shows us that the key to permanent healing is to close doors to disempowering timelines through reconciliation and release of negative emotions, thoughts, and beliefs. We must create new pathways to much happier and more balanced timelines.

In these two client examples, it's pretty obvious that alternate timelines can have a huge impact on our lives. The effect can be either positive or negative, depending on what we are interacting with within those scenarios.

The clear understanding of how the consciousness of one soul weaves through many timelines can assist you in managing your world in a proactive and healthier way. Timeline management can be beneficial to your life and the lives of those around you. In my experience, timeline management can change one's life in the most profound way!

I am going to go out on a limb here. I cannot prove this, but I believe the radio station with the timelines connected to planet Earth has a strong emotional component. In other parallel timelines, in other parts of the multiverse, emotion may be less of a factor. I believe many of us live on other planets, or other universes, in simultaneous timelines where emotional density is less dense than it is here on Earth.

However, if we are dealing with similar circumstances in another universe, those experiences can then energetically filter down into this reality and stimulate our emotions and thoughts here in this timeline without our awareness or understanding of why we are feeling what we are feeling. This idea is tricky to explain but I think Earth's timelines are all about emotional intelligence and this is where we can get tied up with repeating emotional patterns. Other human timelines connected to other parts of the cosmos may not be so emotionally dense. Thinking back to my client who was suffering from grief, losing his female loved one in two timelines simultaneously, he seemed less emotional in the alternate timeline than he did in this one. For some reason that I can't completely understand or even explain with any accuracy, all the grief was flowing in this Earth's timeline. Is this coincidental? I think not. The Earth Matrix seems so emotionally charged. It is here on this planet where we sort out all our emotional baggage as a soul, and so this is where many timelines can converge.

Let's use this example to illustrate my point. The movie you are watching stirs you emotionally at the sad parts, but when you head home back to your normal life, the movie memories and emotions fade away. The movie only affects you for the time that you watch it because you don't currently have a relationship with sadness in your overall life. However, if you are experiencing something in your life that makes you sad - such as a loved one being sick, or struggling with similar themes as the movie - suddenly the movie you watch stirs your unfinished business. Going to a sad movie while you are experiencing sadness in your life is an experience that will cause you more timeline trouble. You are better off to go and watch something funny instead, to counteract what you are feeling in this timeline. In a small, unobvious way, watching a funny movie is helping you shift timelines from sad to funny.

You can manage your timelines to change your daily experiences. Some of the timelines that you are experiencing here on Earth can be very intense, while in other timelines, things are just what they are; you experience them more from an observer's view. However, what you may not be processing in other timelines can unconsciously flow towards you here in this timeline and can become the 'straw that broke the camel's back'. Some intertwining timelines can sink you and others may just fade away. It's all dependent on what affinities and magnetics you might have to specific patterns. This is why it's necessary to navigate where you are putting your attention on a daily basis; your attention and focus on specific themes opens doorways to similar parallel timelines.

My guidance suggests that different timelines serve different purposes and are experienced differently by different people. In this current timeline on Earth, we are experiencing many timelines running simultaneously which may have emotional similarities. In some timelines, there may be a predominant mental component. In other timelines, the focus may be on the spiritual aspect. It's comforting to know that not every timeline is emotional, especially for emotional people who are deep feelers, like I am. For me, it can be a blessing to sync up with a thinker's timeline that has less emotion. But for the over-thinkers of the world, syncing up to a mental timeline could be a real challenge. The key to balance is to figure out what broadcast we are sending out, versus what broadcast we want to receive.

My observation, over a decade of client work, is that many people have a lot of emotional balls in the air that they are trying to juggle. Others are handling only one or two, which is easy to manage. The most emotional people on Earth are the ones experiencing more emotional timelines at once. Less emotional people may be living fewer emotional lives simultaneously.

Unless you can sit down and map how many timelines you are living in - and the nature of those timelines - you really cannot know what you are truly evolving through. Whatever you are moving through can be huge, so it's ok, as a human living on emotional Earth, to cut yourself some slack. Each and every human, including you, is a powerful juggler living a profoundly mysterious life.

CHAPTER 5

Timelines, Past Lives, and the Collective Timeline Influence

The brain doctors suggest memories are not stored in the brain, so my next obvious question is, "Where are memories stored?" I believe all our emotional and thought-based memories are stored within morphic fields of the personal light body, which are encapsulated within a higher dimensional soul energy barrier that includes the Higher Self-consciousness. This personal matrix field can communicate with other fields, depending on the wiring and consciousness of that soul. Within this field are the memories directly related to this unique and authentic soul, where perhaps multiple timelines are running, simultaneously. This is also where the emotional energy is stored in connection with previous incarnations where death and the transformation of the physical body have already taken place. Some say we live in the astral dimension, or heaven, after we die. Or perhaps we simply access, through our light body communication, a field of consciousness where all memories of all living beings have been stored – what I would call a 'Human Collective'. Maybe we exist wherever the divine mind of our soul guides us to be, and we are not limited to just one place in time like the astral dimension.

The astral dimension may be a field of consciousness where

great wisdom is stored. When intuitive people say they are accessing past life memories, I believe they have the ability to interact with those morphic fields that contain both past life information and alternate timeline information. What they are accessing depends on what radio station they are choosing to dial into; each broadcast is at a different level of frequency and consciousness. What is exciting about this, is that the bigger part of us has the ability to inner-relate to a larger 'all knowing' consciousness. This gives us great hope as we learn to master timeline management. This is the Timeline Shifting and Jumping that the gurus we have idolised in the past were able to understand and engage in.

As a shamanic practitioner, I was trained to use trance states to access different communication fields from a deeper place of consciousness. In my sessions, I used trance states to be able to see past lives connected to the soul I was working with. For me, it was the process of using a rattle or a drum to trance out and dial into the morphic fields of stored information located within the light body of that person to witness first-hand details of past incarnations. I visualized the different types of storage as a book case. The closest information on the bookshelf is parallel timelines. We have to climb higher up the book case and into higher frequencies to access past life information. I find past lives take a little more time and a higher frequency to access than alternate timelines.

Or another great visual is that we are like nesting dolls. Simultaneous timelines are the smallest dolls located closest to this incarnation, and the large nesting dolls that are much further out from this incarnation are related to past lives. The further out, the less relatable the information may be, but it's important to note, it is available to flow to us if there is a trigger. Some souls may have information flowing to them related to the age of the 1600's while still living in this 21st-century timeline. There can be interaction within the Human Energetic Communication Field (as illustrated in the picture located before chapter 1).

Another important factor that I have noticed over the many years I have worked with clients is that parallel time lines seem to have emotions attached, and past lives just have information.

For many years when I was a psychic reader, I wondered why, when I worked with some clients doing intuitive readings, I would have emotions flow through me and with other clients I didn't feel anything. Sometimes, with the clients who usually had extremely emotional readings, during other sessions with the same client, there would be no emotions during their readings. I now understand the difference. During my intuitive readings, I was accessing not just past life information but also parallel timeline information. The more emotional readings were, the more likely it was that they were connected to parallel timelines only.

I also feel that some people who can access different timelines more often than others are proficient timeline managers. Some even have the gift to *remember* that they are shifting or jumping timelines. People who have déjà vu, people who remember their dreams and people who have a 'knowing' of future timelines are proficient timeline managers.

Some timeline shifters are good at it, while other people just fall into the timeline mystery without knowing they are doing it because of how their Human Energetic Communication Field works.

I have one female family member who is very sensitive, and I feel she is one of those people who can engage in many timelines simultaneously. She has a huge ability to recall previous emotional experiences. She knows all the details and can describe the senses she'd felt when something dramatic happened to her, for example, when she was a child. She seems to hang onto this information quite clearly, but I also feel she has a lot of emotional experiences going on in other timelines that flow into this one. I have witnessed her personality change right in front of my eyes, and my sense is she had jumped timelines as I witnessed the change. She is normally a gentle and kind person, but I have seen her become very cranky very quickly. One such time was when she had been given strong opioids for pain management after a major surgery. The nurses said she was experiencing this abrupt change in personality due to the drug side effects, but my sense was the drugs took down the veils between timelines. Another timeline, where she is a little less easy going, started to spill into this timeline. She suggested it was her deceased mom coming through her, but I knew it was her consciousness from another timeline flowing into this one. I could sense similarities through her style of verbiage.

I look back over the years that I spent time with her, and I have witnessed abrupt and extreme moodiness. I believe this change in personality is connected to other timeline interactions where she is not such a happy person. I believe she might live in more difficult circumstances in those timelines than this one.

It's hard to decipher this bigger soul view when we are the ant in the ant hill. Unless we can directly relate, it's hard to understand what might be going on right next door in the café (in another timeline). Sometimes we can experience the unexplainable through personal timeline communication.

My intuitive thought is that if we have predominant ways of thinking and predominant beliefs we operate from, then we have doorways to similar alternate timelines. Those timelines may be ours, or they may be connected to the Human Collective. I believe our core beliefs dictate what timelines we access more often.

To illustrate my point, my female family member often speaks about 'being ok'. I think in other timelines she struggles to be ok. Perhaps survival is on the top of her to do list in alternate timelines or perhaps she has struggled in past lives to survive. I am not sure which, but there seems to be a persistent theme in her life that she is 'doing ok'. And when she is not doing ok, many parallel timelines spill into this one, and she becomes overburdened with fear and negative thinking.

From what I have shared to this point, it's pretty obvious that we are far more intricate beings than we know. We have some powerful unseen influences in our life that can affect us in profound ways. We likely have access to thousands of personal timelines, plus access to the multitude of collective timelines we are all connected to; the access becomes exponential!

Now we are going to take one more step up in the nesting dolls example and speak about collective timelines. This subject is where things get very interesting! Let's just think for a minute about past events and the emotional energy that is involved with global events involving large volumes of people. Think of past events such as Atlantis sinking, WWI, WWII, Hiroshima, 9-11 and the destruction of the World Trade Centers, the Indian Ocean tsunami of 2004 and the Japanese tsunami of 2011. All these events involved huge numbers of human casualties. Anyone who was directly impacted by these events, and who is still living today on this side of the veil, likely has within their light body a doorway to all the emotional memories of these events that took place and that are stored in a collective field that is directly connected to the Earth itself. Depending on these people's other timelines and the emotional themes involved, these traumas can either be manageable or not. If the 'tragic themed' doorway is opened wide enough, that person can be flooded with emotions and thoughts that are not theirs but are tied to others who were involved in similar circumstances. Many souls living on Earth at the same time will influence us without our even knowing it. I refer to this principle as the 'Human Collective Timeline' influence. This scenario can either work for us or against us depending on the situation that is unfolding and how we choose to manage things. We can close doorways to this collective by shifting our focus (as described in the examples coming later in this chapter).

Any time humankind has experienced a large death toll, like the 2004 Indian Ocean tsunami, the shock waves of grief went out to anyone who had experienced grief before. Some people would have been profoundly impacted by those difficult emotions and others may have just felt something minor, even undetectable, and moved on. The intensity of each person's reaction would be directly dependant on many factors. However, two big influences would be alternate timelines running with similar themes and grief connected to past lives. If you had, in this time, an active doorway to such themes, then perhaps you felt the extreme pain of thousands of people who just lost loved ones in that natural disaster.

I felt the effects of the tsunami event before it even took place. I was a working psychic at the time. I was often peering into the future timelines for my clients so I had a strong personal connection to what was yet to unfold in the world of creation in connection to Earth's timelines. I had a strong connection to where deceased spirits dwell because I was also working as a medium. Two days before that 2004 earthquake and tsunami hit, I felt an increase in fatigue, and I felt overt grief hit me out of the blue. I said to my husband, "Something is coming, and it's huge!" It took me down fast physically, and I knew it involved emotional energy.

I know now that my past life connection to Atlantis sinking was my large doorway for this difficult energy from the tsunami incident to flow to me. (I also have an affinity for the construct of grief which I will explain later in this chapter.) I am unaware if there are other timelines with similar happenings, but I know my light body makeup allowed that negative energy to flow to me based on my operating system and my past life patterns.

After the event, and the difficult outpouring of emotional grief after that devastating tsunami, it took me about a week to get back on my feet. If I had gone the mainstream route, I likely would have been diagnosed with some strange virus that took me out. I felt flu-ish and extremely fatigued. I was nauseated and very sad. The emotions were very real, and so I had to process them as though I was living it firsthand. Once the tsunami happened, I at least understood what was happening to me. Until the news of the tsunami reached us, I was concerned because I went down so hard and the unexplained sadness was so intense.

If anything hits you hard, and you cannot understand it, then my suggestion is to look for a theme that you might relate to in connection with the collective of human consciousness. All emotions and thought patterns that you experience overtly can have a connection with the bigger consciousness that is not personal. There may be doorways you can close to eliminate those difficult influences. Again we go back to the importance of timeline management processes, which I will highlight in part two of this book.

I want to share one of the most dramatic examples of the personal timeline and Human Collective influences that I saw in my career. I remember getting a call from a mom who was at her wits end regarding her young 6-year-old son who was constantly expressing extreme separation anxiety. She was struggling to get him to assimilate into school because he was struggling to leave her side. His anxiousness was not a learned behaviour because this child demonstrated separation anxiety as a baby. He always had to be held, or he would become unreconcilable in his distress. I sat with the little boy and asked him to tell me his story using little stones. The story he depicted with the stones showed me he felt separated from his loved ones, even as they sat beside him. I asked him to tell me about each stone, and when he began to speak about his people his description did not match this timeline. His mother gave me the strangest look as he described his loved ones. They were very similar looking to his people of this timeline, but the other details did not fit. He didn't give me enough details to know what I was dealing with but I felt he was suffering from a past life memory that was haunting him. I asked him to take me on a journey. With his mom by his side, he allowed me to hold his hand while I used a rattle to take myself into a trance. I was able to connect to his soul, and I was intuitively shown a video of a disturbing tragedy where he and his family were being physically pushed onto an old train car. Then, the picture in my mind changed, and I saw him and his mother being unloaded from the train. I noted they were holding on tight to one another. His mother was frantically calling for the rest of her family members as the little boy clung to her. Then suddenly I saw this horrific scene where the boy was ripped from his mother's arms and she was violently pushed down. He was taken to another location, and she was funneled into a separate cell. I remember the huge pain in my chest while viewing this tragedy and I remember the tears flowing down my face. As I was pulling myself out of the trance, I heard the words, "He never saw his mother again once he entered this concentration camp." I knew he was part of the horrific Jewish story that unfolded in Europe during WWII.

It was clear that this boy had a personal doorway to a very dark time which was influencing this life in a very difficult way. He had huge fear and anxiety based on this previous incarnation. He believed if he could hold on tightly to his mother, he would never lose her, and she would never be harmed. At that point, it made sense to me why he struggled when someone put him down as a baby. His history was impacting him unconsciously, but so was a Human Collective connected to the Nazi Germany story that had huge emotional energy attached to millions of people who were similarly affected.

That was not the only influence this little boy was dealing with. There are other current timelines where this type of tragedy is going on and active in the modern world. If you think of what has happened in Syria, for example, that similar story is unfolding. This little boy was sinking from both the pain of a previous life and also from the fear others are feeling today in a similar scenario. His doorway to this experience allowed him to have connections to other timelines where intense fear and negative experiences flowed.

My only course of action was to help him close that doorway

so all similar timelines, including the personal and the collective influences, would stop haunting him. During his session I had his mother hold him while he cried out the sadness. This helped close the door to that lifetime. Then I got him to visualize a new story where he and his family escaped and were able to get away and find the freedom to live happily ever after. The new story was the best way to assist him to tie into another collective, one that was focused solely on hope and options. It was the best way to stop the momentum of the tragedy that was affecting him unknowingly.

I asked the boy to do an exercise each day for 21 days. He was to draw pictures of what 'hope' looked like for him. It is said that it take 21 days to change a behavior. This exercise would help him shift his mental communication pattern from 'fear' to 'hope'.

His mother phoned me a week later and shared with me that he had settled right down and she was able to leave his side more and more each day. She thanked me for the huge shift she was seeing in him. I shared with her that giving him an avenue to release any unseen negative emotional energies would be the best healing approach she could take with him in future. I also reminded her not take anything at face value because we are intricate beings living in a multiverse scenario.

As a mystic educator, when I hear about people's suffering from something unexplained, my first questions are, "What is energetically stored in their Human Energetic Communication Field within their light body? What possible timelines might be spilling into this one at this moment?" In my experience, I know people are never broken, they just need to be reset from the influences that are not helping them maintain a happy and healthy life. The best step we can take personally is to close doorways that don't serve us and unhook ourselves from the Human Collective of suffering that might be informing us. The Human Collective packs a punch, especially when we relate to negative experiences that millions of other people have a relationship with.

We humans relate even when we don't know we are doing it.

Think about drawing a picture of a sunset. Maybe you draw land at the bottom of the picture, then you illustrate the sea capped by a horizon line and above that is the beautiful picture of the sunset with lots of colours painted through the clouds. This picture brings pleasure to you.

Others might draw a sunset picture just a little bit different from yours, but the idea of a sun set is relatable amongst humans. That picture informs you of something that pleases most people. We all have a collective memory of what a beautiful sunset might look like, and that memory activates within us emotions and senses. Some people can go as far as taste the salt and feel the breeze while drawing, if they are very creative people. Everyone's version of the sunset is unique, but it is still similar between humans.

That sunset picture is a great example of a positive, collectively shared experience. But, as stated above, there are also negative collective experiences that can be event driven or can have themes related to something difficult - like the experience of living with cancer – and suddenly we all have a similar cancer picture. The collective relationships are tricky and can be a difficult part of being energetically connected to a Human Collective. The story and experience of cancer are a difficult one for so many. Cancer has been one of the leading causes of death in our modern times. There is a huge human population suffering from cancer, which makes the impact from cancer in a relationship with the Human Collective level all that much more difficult to unplug from. We have become a large collective of sick people, and there is a lot of emotional energy tied up at the collective level where millions of people are connecting to the cancer story every year. If you were to think of drawing a cancer picture, you might depict a hospital bed, a cat scan, an IV bag for treatment and maybe you would include your loved one showing their physical decline as they journey through the disease. Most people would draw similar things on their pictures.

The minute we can relate to similar cancer stories, we know we have a collective timeline running where cancer is the main theme. The minute someone says we have the cancer disease a personal doorway is opened to that collective. It's not a positive scenario, unless we can choose to change the cancer radio station which we are being informed by.

I had a client contact me to do a distance healing on her. I intuitively knew right away she was dealing with breast cancer. As soon as I sat down and connected with her light body to read her Human Energetic Communication Field, breast cancer was flashing like a neon sign. I spoke with her, and she confirmed that this was why she had contacted me. But I also felt there was something bigger going on that was affecting her. I closed my eyes, and I saw that she was surrounded by the energy of breast cancer. This didn't make sense to me until I asked her about it. She told me she was the program coordinator for breast cancer fundraising and awareness events in her local rural area, and this was her full-time work.

I know lots of people who work in the medical field who never get any of the diseases they are supporting, so I knew somehow she had a personal doorway that was tying her to the collective of breast cancer illness. At that point, I chose to journey to see what was causing the disease connection. When I went back in time to a past life, I saw her as a very young beautiful woman who was married. She was wearing clothes similar to the dress of the 1940's. I heard from my guidance that she had got a lump in her breast and the doctor removed her breast. Her husband turned away from her because he could not face the physical consequences of her surgery. He became an unfaithful man. She died a few years later from both the disease and a broken heart. She was very angry at her death and could not forgive cancer or her husband.

Once I saw this, I came back out of my trance and asked her if she was angry about the disease. Her answer was YES. She shared with me that she had witnessed many injustices in this lifetime and breast cancer was the cause.

I knew another lifetime experience caused her cancer doorway, but the fuel that caused her disease to grow was energetically connected to a larger collective of women experiencing something similar in this current time. She shared with me that her predominant experiences with those she served was surrounded by the energy of anger. She seemed to be stuck on that timeline and once she realised it, she (a non-emotional presenting woman) began to cry and was able to release her pain.

After the emotional release took place, she was able to shift her timeline. We discussed the upside of the disease that she had witnessed over the years in her work. She did say the disease had the ability to change people's lives for the better. She spoke of women leaving unhealthy marriages and women finding a new way of looking at life once diagnosed. These were just a few examples of the positivity she had seen. I told her to start writing down some of the most positive examples and to read them every day. Her new approach was to focus on the upside potentiality, rather than on the side of anger that had been consuming her and was the catalyst for the disease beginning to grow in her.

As a healer, I knew her tragic past life influenced what timelines she was experiencing both personally and in connection with the Human Collective. If you think for a minute of all the women who have felt anger in connection with breast cancer, there is a lot of energy flowing there! She needed to energetically disconnect from that energy.

When I tracked her future after her timeline switch, I saw her as an old woman rallying the women to make the changes they needed to make in their lives. Her timeline had shifted to a positive outcome, rather than a negative one, because she released emotional energy and changed her timeline by focusing on a new radio station.

The key for everyone who is diagnosed with any disease is to find a way to unhook from the disease influence itself and find new ways to relate to it in the most positive way possible. That way they are not tying into bigger, more impactful timelines that can negatively impact them.

You must make a shift to untie yourself from the humans that are suffering through a similar circumstance. Misery loves company, but you do not want to commune with that misery. You must also clear the doorway that allowed the energy to flow in the first place and you must change your story. When you do that, your timelines will shift. I have included some clearing practices in part two of this book that you can use to assist in shifting the influences that are negatively affecting you today.

I have had some lung issues over my lifetime that most would define as asthma. I do my best never to say, "MY asthma". Instead I remind myself that the dis-ease in my lungs is reminding me to keep undoing any emotional traumas that may show up in connection with my childhood and upbringing. Should past life traumas show up in my dreams, I must release those as well. The lung disease is energetically connected to unhealed grief. While I was in-vitro, my mom suffered a huge tragedy with the sudden death of her father. He was her world and when he died her world ended as she knew it. I was energetically imprinted with my mom's emotional grief. I was born a month early and put into an incubator for 30 days because I could not breathe on my own. I began my life filled with grief. So yes, I was an open conduit for grief energy to impact me.

Earlier in this chapter I shared that I had an overt physical and emotional response prior and during the 2004 Indian Ocean tsunami event. The grief connected to that event flowed to me through my grief doorway. I have an affinity to the construct of grief, which has allowed that grieving collective to influence me. Luckily, with my experience, years of study and practising my healing techniques, I have been able to release grief timelines and continually work on closing the doorway to grief. This has helped me improve my lung capacity immensely. I no longer suffer from yearly pneumonia or bronchitis. I have found every time something shows up in my life around the theme of grief, I can process and shift my radio stations a little clearer each time.

Another way to state this is that the incremental shifts I have made have allowed me to jump out of an illness timeline into a well-being timeline because I am tending to the underlying cause of the original illness. It's working for me. My body is responding to the more positive timeline.

Healing is always possible once you understand what you need to do to shift the energetic influences, which then will allow a natural healing response to take place.

CHAPTER 6

Accessing Alternate Timelines to Create a Better Life

I believe every emotional experience that happens on Earth creates a timeline of some sort. I believe little bursts of information are stored in both the matrix of the person having the experience, and in the Earth's matrix. I also believe large events that have continuous emotional energy feeding back into the timeline will create a bigger, more detailed timeline. The simplest way I can describe it is that there are little insignificant timelines that may never be accessed again, and there are bigger timelines that store large amounts of information that are accessed by many, often. The size or impact of the timeline is directly relative to the number of people emotionally and mentally fuelling that timeline.

When a human walks to the fridge and forgets what they are doing, perhaps the little timeline they shifted into is just slightly different than the timeline they normally access, and so it's insignificant. However, if something big in the timeline they access takes place that is outside of the normal events of a person's life - something like a wedding - that timeline would make a bigger impact.

That wedding timeline has a lot of emotional details and people who are attached to it, so it stays in the forefront of the newly wed's awareness. If we use the nesting doll example, that wedding timeline would be located close to the person during the planning of the wedding, throughout the wedding event and directly after the wedding. However, over time, the past wedding experience would be less of a focus and that timeline would slowly be moved out to the outer layers of the person's light body. It becomes a memory that is slowly forgotten. However, if someone takes out their wedding album to look at the photos, they would bring that timeline closer to them and reactivate the information that is stored within that timeline.

Older emotional events, such as the fall of Atlantis or the decline of matriarchal-based societies, have a lot of emotion and thoughts stored within the Earth's matrix in direct relationship with these negative shifts. However, there was also a time when these golden eras were flourishing, and greatness bestowed the Earth and all who dwelled here. What this means is that the timeline of greatness still exists and is therefore still accessible. It's a big timeline, and there are lots of details in that timeline; we have to fine tune the doorway to that timeline for the specifics we seek to flow back to us. We do that by focusing on smaller details that we desire.

Most people seek a similar life. They want happiness, health, a nice place to live. They value family. They desire access to money to buy things that they need or desire. In general, people want to live a fulfilling life. Unfortunately, over a declining shift of ages, we have forgotten that we are the DJs in our lives. Our amnesia has caused us to live out the programs of a general populous and the bigger timelines that have a consistent theme. We are constantly dialing into radio stations that don't help us or provide for us. Instead, those radio stations hinder us.

During meditations, I have been told by my divine guidance that we currently live in a very competitive collective timeline fuelled by a deep sense of scarcity. The idea that there is never enough to go around drives us to believe - and emotionally fuel the thought - that there is never enough money, or love, or health, or safety. We live without many of the ways of life we deserve. Somewhere, we have faulty, negatively-based timelines informing us, and it causes us unnecessary suffering.

In 2007, the movie **The Secret** was released, and its message relating to the law of attraction was hugely appealing to the general populace. It was a great introduction to the idea that we have influence over what we create in our lives. However, this movie did not address the idea of the unhealable wound from other timelines that unknowingly influence what we can and cannot create.

The message in the movie about manifesting a car advised you to sit and visualize what you want for a car and then feel what it would feel like to drive that car. The difficulty with that idea is that perhaps there are timelines in your Human Energetic Communication Field that block you from manifesting your desire and therefore the car will never appear. In this case, your personal timelines do not necessarily support what you are seeking. You fail to manifest what you want and therefore add more negative emotions to the timeline theme of 'lack'.

My clients who sought my services always knew there was something they struggled to reset. Personally, I believe we all have themes that block us from living the perfect life. However, we do have the ability to refocus and realign to open doorways to timelines that we seek. We also have the ability to refocus to access collective timelines where greatness exists. Collective timelines can trump personal timelines because they can have more energy and momentum.

The key is we must do some personal work to change our radio stations so that we can attract and create from a desirable doorway.

Esther Hicks channels a higher dimensional consciousness known as Abraham. Abraham's teachings have become extremely popular over the decades through Esther's books and through her sharing of Abraham's wisdom at live gatherings. I have been a student of her teachings for many years because I love the results her practical wisdom provides. I believe through her 'law of attraction' principle and related teachings, Esther is helping people to understand that we are truly responsible for what we create in our lives and that we do have an influence on how our lives will unfold.

If positive thinking creates positive lives and people become more positive thinkers, then this movement can positively impact the Human Collective in a profoundly positive way. I feel Esther Hicks and Abraham are changing the world by shifting millions of people from default 'manifesters' to deliberate co-creators.

As a healer and a mystic, I have always wanted to understand the mechanics of the law of attraction and the idea of parallel time lines fills in the gaps for me.

Abraham always speaks about slowing down the negative thinking momentum and increasing the positive thinking momentum to influence co-creation in the direction we seek, to prevent drawing what is unwanted into our lives. The idea of momentum is important because momentum affects what timeline we are drawing from personally and collectively. We have lived many lives, and likely we have lived both positive and negative-themed experiences. The personal timelines we want to access are the ones that fuel positive ideas and energy into this timeline.

All similar emotional energy - of both positive and negative experiences on Earth - is stored in the Earth's matrix. This energy is accessible to you as long as you open doorways to that information and magnetics. Your personal timelines create the first doorway which will naturally link to the collective doorway with the same theme. When you connect to a large collective timeline, lots of momentum can flow back to you and affect your magnetics to fuel what you seek. You are in a symbiotic relationship with the 'All that has ever happened on Earth', based on your personal connections to the Earth Matrix itself.

Some gurus say that what happens to the "One" happens to the 'All'. It's true. As a human, you are in communication with multiple timelines simultaneously, and all timelines can have a direct impact on your life.

The important point I must make here is that to be a successful co-creator, you must manage your personal timeline doorways. Doorway management begins by becoming honest with how you operate in the world; by asking yourself the tough questions. What type of emotions and thoughts do you have on a daily basis that feed similar energy back into your life? What type of 'garden' are you growing? Are you planting good seeds that will provide a bountiful harvest? Or are you planting negative weeds? Are you a positive thinker or do you get drawn into negative ideals and beliefs? Are you hanging out with a positive thinking collective or communing in the negative arena?

Once you figure out your major timelines and how you are creating from them, you can make the adjustments needed to shift things in the direction you seek. Part two of this book will provide exercises that will assist you in shifting to the most beneficial timeline for you. You will also learn to tweak timelines as you go.

I close this chapter with the exciting announcement that all collective timelines are now accessible to all of humanity. This was not always the case. Humanity has been reliving difficult timelines over and over again, unable to break free from our suffering. However, the predicted shift of 2012 did point to the fact that something has changed in our cosmic landscape; something has opened up. The ideals of a golden age have been unlocked and can now influence us in the most beneficial ways.

It truly is an exciting time to be alive!

PART 2

Consciously Shifting Timelines

CHAPTER 7

Earth Matrix is the Bridge

The way to consciously shift timelines is to create a bridge between this timeline that you find yourself in now and the one that you seek. The bridge cannot be too long, or it will not work. Another way to say this is, you cannot have too much of a stretch in frequency between one timeline and another. I have not talked about frequency before now, but frequency is the foundation of Timeline Shifting.

Personal frequency is in direct relationship with how we think and how we feel. If you feel good and happy, your frequency is running higher then when you feel down and depressed.

When you feel down, you are experiencing a need for balance. Immediate action is advised. Ignoring things does not work! When your frequency becomes lower than normal, there can be 'unhealed, ignored feelings' creeping in. Unhealed feelings can be the 'straw that broke the camel's back.'

The best approach for closure and permanent healing is to bring healing to the wounded parts of you. This will release the emotional pressure that has built up over time. It's important to note that the older the energies are, the more attention they may need. Often old emotions mean stuffed emotions and it takes some gentle coaxing to bring them to the surface. It's to your benefit to meet the stories that cause you the most suffering with love and compassion.

If you want things to improve in your life, you must build a higher frequency bridge to where you want to go. The best way to build a bridge is to shift how you are feeling in the here and now to a higher frequency. The way to do that is to shift the negative momentum you find yourself caught in.

In my shamanic world, we would say we need to close one door and open another door where new, higher frequency energies exist. However, healing is always needed before a door is closed abruptly.

To address the concept of shifting your negative momentum, go back to the picture of the Human Energetic Communication Field. You notice how the 'Earth Matrix' sits between the 'Mental Thoughts and Emotions' field and the 'Parallel Timeline' field. This communication model is only active when you have incarnated as a physical being on Earth. When you die and pull your life force from this planet, your communication field within your light body will reset to another model that will not include the Earth Matrix.

The Human Energetic Communication Field can have incredible influence on us if we dial into that specific radio station, since the Earth Matrix contains codes of healing. The matrix of the Earth also fuels the outcome of personal and global fulfilment. This matrix provides for everyone who lives on this planet. The key question is, "What seeds are we planting in this matrix, both personally and collectively?"

This planet Earth teaches us to master our thoughts and emotions. In the past, it might have taken 1,000 incarnations to become masters, but things are changing as we wake up to our co-creational gifts and begin to know ourselves and our power.

I believe we, as a human race, have been looping through a negative pattern of thinking for a long time. It's all about to change with the new cosmic energies that are reigning down on Earth. Earth's energy field is becoming more charged, and this means we will be able to access more power to heal ourselves and create new uplifting experiences in our lives. We will be able to create, with accuracy, the bridges needed for the timeline shifting that we seek.

The key to living a powerful co-creative life is to find a way to shift how you feel so you can open doorways to alternate timelines that have good vibes within. The Earth Matrix is the answer to shifting your frequency. The Earth Matrix can help you build the new bridges to where you want to be in your co-creational timelines. The Earth Matrix and its availability to assist you is the most powerful source you can touch, taste and feel while in physical form.

Earth traditions have been successfully practiced for so long on Earth because the rituals and practices consistently work to improve life. Shamans work within the Earth Matrix to shift reality and help their clients shift their communication fields to a more positive frequency. Without utilizing the Earth's matrix, we can lack the physical energy needed to manifest the outcomes that we desire.

Take active steps each day to connect with the Earth Matrix to keep your personal timeline upbeat, such as: enjoy a walk in nature; carry stones in your pockets; meditate against a tree; or whatever action connects you with Earth energy.

CHAPTER 8

Dream Time Investigation

To learn what needs to be shifted and healed in your life, you need to understand the outside lower frequency influences that may be impeding you. The most masterful way to understand what is spilling into your world is to monitor your dream time. Your dreams are guiding you in a very important way.

If you do not remember your dreams, it may be because the frequency in your bedroom needs to be elevated. You need a high frequency in your bedroom to help you hold onto the memories as you awaken and create a bridge between your dream time and waking time. Here are a couple of hints on how to increase the retention of your dream memories.

- Place a salt or selenite lamp in your bedroom to continuously cleanse any negative energies.
- Shut down all unnecessary electronics in your bedroom while sleeping.
- Diffuse pure essential oils, like lavender, which will help calm your nervous system while your body rests.
- Place a saltwater cleansed, clear quartz crystal underneath your pillow. Cleanse it often. This will amplify the ability to retain memories.

- Write down any memories from your Dreamtime right away, even if they don't make sense. It doesn't matter if you understand at the beginning. It matters that you are creating a consistent pattern of memory recall.
- If you are a believer in soul guides and angels, ask them for help in remembering your soul guidance. Requesting help opens up a doorway of support.
- Practice a breathing technique that helps you relax before you go to sleep. For example, the 4-7-8 breathing technique, where you breath in through your nose to the count of 4, hold your breath for 7 counts and then slowly exhale through your mouth for 8 counts. Five rounds of this breathing pattern will help you relax and sleep.
- Set the intention to receive more information.

Once you begin writing down your dreams, notice if you have a theme running in your dreams that you can relate to in your life. If yes, then you have direct information coming through your dream time guiding you to what you might be experiencing on alternate timelines.

If you are having random dreams, then look at the similarities of the theme of your entertainment, such as shows, movies or books you are reading. If there is a similarity to those influences, stop engaging with that theme of entertainment for a few days to see if your dreams change.

Often we 'seed' our consciousness with the emotional experiences we relate with through our entertainment choices. Entertainment can interfere with the clarity of our dreams. The key is to shift the outside influences to a neutral place. Then we can discern what our Higher Self and soul is guiding us with through our dream time communication.

Dream time monitoring, with some practice and commitment, can give you a great deal of information about what might be unfolding for you in alternate timelines. Monitoring your dreams might also reveal what is found within your unconscious mind that you still have to work through emotionally. Sometimes you are given a chance, through your dream experiences, to let off some emotional steam in this reality, which is always a beneficial thing. Letting go of emotions always lends to helping yourself maintain balance on this side of the veil, where we know emotions can be more intense. Release of negative emotions and thought also makes way for you to build new bridges in a more positive frequency. Dumping anchors helps your 'soul boat' sail.

The key is, if something from dream time upsets you, release it. In the following chapters, I share a few practices to help you release emotion and negative energy.

CHAPTER 9

Water Release Process to Shift Frequency

Water is a powerful, earth-based element that can assist humans in releasing emotional and mental energy when the momentum of negativity takes hold of our thoughts. Masaru Emoto's work, which was published in his book, *"Hidden Messages in Water"* proves that we have energetic ties to water. His study and work showed that written words have either a positive or negative impact on the structure of water, depending on the nature of the words used. The results of his study provide great news for humans who want to shift negative momentum and reset to a more positive timeline.

If you look back to the picture of the Human Energetic Communication Field you will see that we have easy access to the Earth Matrix. Water can be our physical conduit for direct connection to the Earth Matrix. Water will assist us in resetting negativity that is impeding our lives and help us to shift our timelines by building new bridges to timelines when we need it most. I choose the water element over fire because it is easy to access and water can be safely used by children. Water can also be easy to use in the busiest of places, like the downtown metropolis of any big city.

The key to shifting timelines is to stop the negative momentum and take the energetic and emotional pressure off the mind that loops through negative thoughts.

If you have a negative experience that upsets you, grab a glass of tap water and begin to blow the emotional and mental energy into the water. Every time you inhale visualize breathing in the 'all providing cosmic light'. Every time you exhale visualize yourself pushing out and releasing the negative feelings that you are having. Keep doing this process until you no longer have negative thoughts. If you get light headed, pause for a moment. Once the light headedness stops, go back to breathing in the cosmic light and breathing out the negative thoughts and emotions until you feel the negative energy completely subside.

When you are complete with the water release exercise, pour the water on the land, if possible. If you can't pour the water on the land, pour it down the sink. Either approach works; pouring the water on the land allows a deeper healing process to take place because you are directly interacting with the Earth matrix.

Once you have completed your release and disposed of the water, please take a minute to give thanks to the water and to the Earth for her healing support. The act of gratitude assists the finalization of release. To complete your release, cross your arms in front of your heart. Then quickly release your arms to your sides in the act of cutting all ties to the negative energies that you transformed. You should feel a sense of lightness in your being at this point. Take a minute or two to visualize the perfect outcome you want. Then congratulate yourself. You have just intentionally built a bridge to another timeline.

To continue to experience that desired timeline, you must maintain the frequency or personal vibe that you felt at the completion of the release. The lightness of being you feel is a good indicator that you have dumped the heaviness of your current timeline and have advanced upwards to a higher frequency.

Water release is the easiest way to shift your frequency so that you can access other timelines. It's one of my favourite release techniques because I can do it anywhere, anytime without anyone knowing that I am doing it. I choose to whisper my thoughts and blow my emotions into the water very quietly until I can whisper my vision with clarity. While I am quietly communicating, I feel as though I am speaking to the Earth herself. Water is my messenger and my healing ally. I use "I am" statements in my release process. For example, "I am releasing fear" or "I am releasing pain." The emotions you release could also be hurt, anger, sadness, resentment or any combination of these emotions. I may then state my vision as, "I am balanced, happy, harmonious, sacred."

When my father was in the hospital it was a very difficult situation to be a part of. I would keep a jar of water in my car and I would do my release process before I drove home from the hospital every night so I would be in a good space while driving. Plus it was important to me that I had shed all the upset and the hospital energy before I went back to my home life. That way I did not bring negative energy into my home.

This water release technique is a simple and fast timeline management process that anyone can do. The more we release the negative energies that we collect in life, the more energetically positive we can be in our lives. Then through our positive vibrations, it is much easier to be able to directly bridge and communicate with more positive timelines.

CHAPTER 10

Manage Your Environment

It is said that we entrain to our environment energetically, mentally and emotionally. I believe that our physical health and well-being is also dramatically affected by our physical environment. I believe we can encourage, through our actions, a more positive living experience by shifting our approach with those whom we share our environment with. If we take responsibility for how we feel and take actions to shift our radio stations, then no one holds dominion over us.

If we don't feel we are empowered to make changes, then something is out of balance.

Honesty with ourselves is the best policy to become powerful co-creators. We cannot change what we ignore. We also cannot change others. We only have the ability to change our views and our way of reacting to any given situation.

If someone we live with is bringing us down, then we have to find solutions to shift that. Relying on others to make us happy can leave us disappointed, disheartened and disempowered. These three big D's will never provide positivity.

All difficult situations have solutions, and it begins with the ways we think about our situations. Remember, diffusing emotions is the best option. I find if I can diffuse negative energies within myself before I ever react, things go better for me and those I live with.

The best secondary approach is to use power words internally to change the reaction to any given stimuli that negatively impacts you. I often use the words in my head, "It's not my monkey" when someone is acting negatively around me, which helps me shift from a negative reaction to a positive projection of thought within my head. I say, "It's not my monkey" over and over again, reminding myself that how someone else operates is not my business.

Sometimes, I believe it is my role to stay upbeat no matter what. I don't mean to say you should put a happy sticker on a tragedy; I mean everyday life can be a challenge, but you can change how you look at that challenge. It's a choice that no one can take from you, not even the most negative of people.

Another approach I use is to focus on a symbol that represents love to me; then I can drown out the negative that is coming at me. I choose to be the diffuser of the projections that exist around me.

My suggestion to help you manage your environment is to find a phrase that you can say in your head that helps you unplug from any negative projections coming at you, or find a symbol that helps you change your magnetic energy so that you don't get fished into someone else's negative projection. Both of these approaches work well and help to interrupt someone else's negative momentum from affecting you.

The other option, if plausible, is just to leave the environment/ situation that is challenging you. Once you have separated yourself, send loving energy to that person and/or situation. This exit will give you a chance to shift your momentum back to your own vibe. I also suggest that after you leave, you cross your arms in front of your heart and quickly release your arms to the sides with a cutting action. This action will stop the energy drain. Take a few minutes to breathe deeper so that you can calm yourself down.

If you can't leave the situation, or you get sucked into a disagreement or fight, then shift your vibrations afterwards using the water technique. Do what you can to shift the negative momentum so that you can return to your timeline.

Outside influences can dramatically impact us unknowingly, especially if we don't manage our energy fields. I have personally jumped into a negative timeline based on circumstances that I could have managed better.

One night, after a long challenging day of emotional ups and downs, I went to bed feeling depleted. I woke up about three hours later to a violent situation in the hotel I was staying in. I heard glass breaking and people laughing. I could hear and feel the building shake while I lay in my bed vibrating from fear as the violent situation unfolded one floor down. What I kept thinking to myself was, "Why are there no police coming?" It was an old building so I could not get up and walk around without being heard, so I stayed in my bed, holding the crystal I slept with. I began to speak my power words, "I am safe. I am protected. No harm comes to me or anyone else in this place." I also called in some of my power sources to surround me. Eventually, after about 40 minutes, quiet took hold below. I fell back asleep with the crystal in my hand.

I woke up the next morning, still holding the crystal, and I remembered what went on. I texted my husband with the details and prepared for my day.

When I went to leave the hotel, I expected to find the building and property damaged. Instead, nothing was damaged. All was well.

Puzzled, I contacted one of my intuitive friends for insight. He told me he felt I had made a Timeline Jump. He suggested I do some intuitive work around the situation. I did and my guidance suggested that the building had a violent timeline attached. I had allowed my field to become vibrationally depressed that day, which opened the doorway to that negative timeline. It was a great lesson for me to ensure I never let my energy management slip!

CHAPTER 11

Sound

Sound is one of the most powerful personal tools we have. Sound can be used instantly, in nearly any situation to bridge new timelines. Since all matter is made of different frequencies of the manifested quantum field, we have the ability to create a different reality with sound.

Your voice is the intermediary between the worlds of seen and unseen. One of the most effective ways to change your energy field is through working with your voice.

Ancient traditions suggest that everything in the Universe is a manifestation of the sound, "Om". "Om" may be the collective sound of the Universe, the Primordial Sound that we all interconnect to at the level of the soul collective. The seed syllable "Om" causes a certain frequency to imprint upon the matter around it, and thus changes the energetic field in a positive way. Chanting "Om" increases your vibration. Try chanting it yourself. You can even whisper "Om" when you are in a crisis moment; see what unfolds after that.

I have led chants within a group setting, and I find chanting "Om" immediately settles everyone down and synergistically creates a sense of peace and harmony within the group. Chanting power words is easy and works, too.

CHAPTER 12

Creating New Timelines

You are a powerful creator of reality, and your sacred gift to yourself is to recognize you have such power. Over the years people have talked about ways and means to utilize their co-creative energies in which they can positively influence their lives. These very experiences are creating alternate timelines for you to be able to access. Also, the more you move from reaction to a co-creative approach in life, the more influence you will have in your life to sync up to the universal frequencies that provide what you desire.

Vision boards are one of the most powerful tools to influence and open door ways to positive timelines. When humans mix their creative power with their upbeat visions, something wonderful triggers the cosmos.

Vision boards are not a new concept, but perhaps I can add a nuance that will assist in seeing your manifestation come to light faster.

Perhaps you are seeking to find a new home. You choose to cut out pictures of homes very similar to what you like. Maybe you choose colours and furniture, and you place pictures on your board that support your vision and desired creation.

I suggest you add to your vision board by purchasing inexpensive items that would be found in your new home and place them on, or close to, your vision board. Set aside a little manifestation area away from electronics. Perhaps you buy swatches of cloth, or buy a new candle stick holder or find a small coffee table nick-knack that would look good on the furniture you have chosen.

Taking steps and positively charging those actions with upbeat emotions will open door ways to a timeline where that home exists. The more action you take towards the creation of your new home, the more you fuel it to manifest.

Remember, the bridge between timelines cannot be too long or, in other words, you cannot have too much of a stretch in frequency between this timeline and the one that holds your dream home. This means you have to believe the home will take form; what you are envisioning needs to be believable on your part.

The next step to opening your timeline door is to start noticing the subtle changes in your reality that support your new vision. Perhaps through strange circumstances, you are notified of a new community being built just outside the city. You note it and investigate. You like what this new community has to offer, so you add that community name, or a picture of the community, to your vision board.

Then, maybe you are called into your boss' office and told you have qualified for a raise. You will be making more money starting in two weeks. Write that information out on a piece of paper and add it to your vision board.

Perhaps purchase another small item to add to your other items. This will build momentum with your vision.

Keep taking action to add to your vision board through your day-to-day life. You want to keep the doorway open to that timeline by fuelling it with your creative thoughts and positive emotional energy. If you do get any negative thoughts showing up, then use a release technique to get the negative energy out of the way. As other Law of Attraction experts state, you must be in the vibrational match to what you are trying to attract.

My sense is you must keep the bridge clear and the timeline door way open by managing your vibrations, thoughts and feelings in the most positive of ways. Take continuous action to support your vision board, and you will see the cosmic energies align to open door ways to new your timeline opportunities.

IN CLOSING

Timeline Shifting will become a more active practice for humans as the cosmic shift of ages continues. Timeline Shifting will happen with, our without, our awareness. The veils between timelines are becoming thinner, and this means we can more easily access other timelines based on our frequency broadcast. A paradigm shift like we are experiencing also means we have more capability to live the lives we want to live surrounded by desirable circumstances that we can choose. It's a great time to be alive.

Try working with alternate timelines with a little humour and respect and see how your world changes. I have witnessed amazing things unfold in my life, and I know this approach to improving life works. Whatever you do, please remember you chose to incarnate on this planet to learn, grow, and expand. You also came here to enjoy the gifts this planet has to offer. It's a sacred time, and it's time to enjoy an extraordinary life. Happy Shifting!

NOTES

NOTES

NOTES

NOTES

NOTES

NOTES

CPSIA information can be obtained
at www.ICGtesting.com
Printed in the USA
LVOW03s1552241117
557433LV00001B/1/P